Cee:

Anchored in Poetree

Poems by Gwen Cee

By: Gwendolyn M. Pearce

Cee'rum V Publishing

ISBN-13: 978-0692505335
(Cee'rum V. Publishing)

ISBN-10: 0692505334

Published by: Cee'rum V. Publishing
                Louisville, KY

Dedicated to:

To my family, with so much love. I am thankful for every moment we share and am grateful for our daily madness which is what makes our time so special.

My husband, I thank you for trying to teach me how to live in the moment without so much fear and worry and for carrying me through anxiety. I am thankful that you support me so much that you roll with the punches of a changing life after my heightened anxiety.

Just like your father, my sons, each of you hold a place beyond my heart; a place in my soul. I pray for each of you daily. I pray for your protection and your futures. While the turmoil existed, I benefited from the threat that our family faced; carrying that burden for nearly three years ultimately led me to God.

My relationship with Him is one that I have to work on each day but I do so joyfully. I pray that God will continue to guide me and enhance my spirit and my mind and lead me to be the best woman, wife and mother I possibly can.

Please never forget your compassion.
I love you.

"ShowLoveGrowLove"

**And, to any artist or friend who supports me, thank you.
I, especially appreciate the POET love.**

Psalms 34:4 *I sought the Lord, and he answered me and
delivered me from all my fears.*

Contents

Allow Your Eyes to

CEE All Things

"Road Trips"

I grew up on road trips
So the colloquial scrapes and bruises were used to keep
me moving
Monitoring and maintaining
While gaining.........A Sense...of self
Trying to be deeper than the potholes
That bent my rim
And trying to build my own worth
Because a flat is not an "all is lost"
Unless it's a flat line; a permanent pause
Of my heart
Until then.............. I look back...
But no regrets...
Knowing I could have been better:
"No fighting"
"Straight to college"
"Increased self-love"
"Less tolerance................. for letdowns"
But that wouldn't make me who I am
In fact I wouldn't be here today
Able to relay
The things that have blown me away
Like lost love
Heightened hurt from unwarranted places
Harmless "harm" from myself
I spent my whole life on high alert and for what?
...because of fear from being hurt?
Strangely dismissing anything that didn't glisten and make
me seem happy?
Back then I'd rather live in fear
and never know
... that was then.

July 13, 2015

"Implement"

To fake not having regret...
Of loss of time; a precious gift,
She instead regress --- es and says...
That it's his...fault...praying that young girls will witness....
Her telling story of time's ability to diminish...

And to take note before that unknown feeling of
emptiness....shows up...
Emptying what was....thought to exist.

See young girls, you must first LIVE YOUR life before you
claim that YOUR "growing" has finished....
Don't get caught up in this or that, "I love him, he loves me"
before your "me" has its own image....

I assure you that you were NOT designed to be his....until
you are first your "OWN."
That means your SELF "known,"
Your goals "grown,"
Your future-not on loan...

Respect expected and graciously accepted, as a lady
should...
No fears of sticks and stones,
Level-headed, swivel shoulders with ability to brush off
nonsense,
Not perfect by any means and not always right...but ability
to design a plan and make a decision without hurdling a
fence...

Ability to say "I'M PLEased that I MEaNT" to know myself
and love me too...before I arranged my world in an
attempt....to breathe life into you.
No need to fake not having regret...
No need to search for time forever gone...
No need to regress.....

When self IMPLEMENT has occurred....my, mine, me,
understanding from within...
To implement is to love yourself. -- first!

To love all that is you so that some random spark doesn't
confuse you, so that some random heart doesn't try to take
your beat, so that some random individual has no
opportunity to view you as residual.

Love all that is you! Your name, your face, your eyes, your
heart, your history, your tears, your spirit, your energy,
your present, your future, your gift (yes, you have one),
your smile, your good, your bad, your light, your dark, your
quiet, your loud, your ashamed, your proud, your rights,
your wrongs, your laugh as you carry on..
Through your life,
Your IMPLEMENT,
Your "I'M PLEased to announce that I MEaNT to be "me.""
And, to live in this wide world, your destiny......

September 30, 2014

"Myth of the Picture"

Picture perfect, no not quite…
Picture perfect, no not quite…
Picture perfect, no not quite, rather trying too hard.

Faceless Picture… leaving me alone… inside
Not one ounce of pleasure,
No joy ride…

Perfect picture…
Driving my new range,
New endeavors…
Picture perfect, slick, smile big
Show'em what they look for,
not what you give
Give thanks! For another day
Glance upon, false memories, choose to let them fade…
Picture perfect – a choice to see, take a peek behind the
eyes
Beyond the rosy cheeks,
What shall future photos be?-Truly happy or bleak?

Picture perfect, staged, drama, smile beyond that of
beginners,
Perfect only IFFFF - living in a world of sinners…
Sin overshadowed by the flash, as long as the photos say
so then it must be….picture perfect

Picture perfect, lacking a heartfelt smile, perfect
picture, with no edits necessary, perfect story, lacking any
real text, text not that of a phone, real conversation,
dialogue, things that create and allow picture perfect to
exist and carry on…

Perfect picture is reality;
It's the perfect shot; J. Dixie
Perfect pictures deliver energy
Picture perfect…

What do you see?
Picture perfect...
I ask you "what do you see?"
Seek and find, move beyond the daily grind,
Picture perfect, perfect picture, don't let the myth get'cha.

Spring 2013

"He is My..."

He's like your car keys or your favorite pair of jeans.
He exists...there are times when he chooses to elude...
When found, he's often colorful, vivid; at others he's faded
like a slowly vanishing bruise

I've seen him brighten up at just the right time when I was
timid and once when I was livid
I love the way he works for me; I trust him deeply,
Although he comes and goes, he supports me in my goals,
I know he will never leave me...completely.

Sometimes he's hard to locate; but he's real; he's visible
I've seen him...Walk into rooms...with so many other
people

He's highly sought after, imminent,
Once someone took him, carried him away in silence
Fate led him back to me; He returned...at just the perfect
moment.

He is pretty amazing, the things he has done for me, he
can do for you...
He can promote you, compliment you, and raise your
standards up.

Firmness exists when he's around, he can remove you
from a rut; release you from that which holds you down,
He's more enduring than luck!
His cousin is not too bad either; he keeps you moving
forward after an "Awh Shucks"
His cousin is courage; He is there to help you endure
Persist, be daring and fearless as you pledge....
To take chances and commit to opening new doors

He's powerful, he fights for my bashful.
He declares; he makes statements; he diminishes doubt...

Says to me "you must choose this or that" when on an
issue I want to straddle,
He does not let me remain idle…

And, I'm never allowed to pout.

He carries some clout; you'll see he can pick you up and
take you out;
When he's ignited, there's no place he can't drive you; if he
crashes, though, literally! Game Over! You're out!

With him, it's a give and take relationship……
If you believe in him, he believes back; he likes to feel
relevant…
He makes me feel worthy of the attention of others; without
my becoming too self-indulgent.
Sometimes he's blocked by childhood memories; using
him is not always easy;

But when I feel like a fiddler on the roof; he knows just
what part of me to fiddle with…my anxiety…
He is wise and I use him wisely.

He tells people that I can be trusted and lets them know we
share similar struggles;
He helps me decide which battles to seek and when to turn
the other cheek.

He can be relied upon; he's been there when I've lost and
he's been there when I've won
Although, I love and prefer hanging out with Modesty;
I know that sometimes I have to use him; include him;
sometimes wear him out when he is already running
thin………because it I fail to do so or deprive him… Of
attention; he might leave; call it quits; or say to me
"Someone else needs my help with their intentions."

I can't let this end because I need him more than any other
trait or character I've known.

He is there when I hurdle a fence, pondering whether the grass might be greener.
He is there when I'm running out of common sense, he has even witnessed some of my ignorance.

He is there when I'm broke; no dollars, just cents, he is there for all of my important events...
I appreciate his permanence,

He lives with me; no rent necessary.

When things are intense...

He suppresses the scary.
He is my Confidence!

Summer 2013

"Played for Foreplay"

I was just reminiscing on how we used to spend time
together; all the time...
How you use to MAKE time for me but you don't do that
anymore...

You stopped that...
Lol at you! Lol at your strong game in its weakest form...
I allowed my mouth to mumble those words,

"I'm so in love with you."

After that, LOUDLY I never seen you much;
There are no rules with my love; except that you must
"accept" it...
I thought you were gone off me but you did not accept my
love...
Even with my waiting around, adhering to your schedule –
you still never...
"accepted" my love.

Lol at your game! But Lol at my slightly naïve self and my
wishful thinking...
Thinking you were falling in love with me...
I misunderstood your love of foreplay, mistaking it as...
A love of kissing, touching and caressing me...
I made a mistake; followed the queues of lust,
Allowed my mind to ride passenger as my heart escalated
out of control...

I thought you were falling in love with me......that I had a
place-
With you...your "lady"............... your future, your "keep
you motivated"
But where I wished to go, you refused to stroll.
I see now, I was not ready for a Gemini,
I was not ready for you; your weed smoke; your low eyes,

I was not ready for the awakening of Gwen's heart because……

WOW! My ability to overanalyze – sure results in making something out of nothing
What US?????????????????

I thought you wanted me to be yours, I wanted to be just that….
I made a lot of out of those wants=Notebook, Spider, Resolution, Corrupted,
These Hands…

But now, I will NOT come over because you ask…
I will not bring a plate, drop a lunch,
bring you a slushy, come watch Sanford & Son…
Follow your patterns and be your "win' on Wednesday…
right after your Tuesday Trick.
Because aftershocks of seeing you; that shit is sick……

I might long for you; envision your face…
A song or poem might highlight a memory of a date…
I own up when I'm wrong about something…
So when I wrote 'coRUPPted,' I said not just a one and done but like the players you represent, that's what we are
– "done."

You were one season, my winter for after my fall…
I would've been your winner after them all…

Cause even when I fall hard, I still get up. Big Blue's Corruption
couldn't hold me,

I'm still surprised that I even let BBN inspire my poetry….
I'm going to give it to the laws of chemistry,
My hearth throbbed; yours didn't----sucks for me,
I'm going to blame it on something greater than "us" the realization that this

"flow exists………… in me."

Thanks for your bite,
Creating the highs, the lows, the torture, the good
adrenaline; making me write….

Thanks for the spark to the heart, eight months of foreplay,
The venom in my veins; as you fulfilled your addiction
through the use of me.

All these words I have written – forget wordplay; nothing
left for us-
"Played by Foreplay" – we must now walk away…
Forget January 1st – It's July 1st- RESOLUTION

Drop the mic, cause spittin about you has the same affects
as using.

June 19, 2014

"Alice"

Because when Andrea Evans-Bennett chased Mr. Cartwright...
She got caught right?
And she could not write...
Or speak.........Or act in a way...
Or do a thing....to change...
The past...... the drama that she created and became a glutton for...
Heart punished by what she thought was love; while becoming estranged...
Him going to his wife, leaving in room 629 traces of her.....
Whore....

What more?
Visits from Chris Bennett...
The overall good dude, now appearing in her eyes as the MAN that he always was...
All along, he could have been "it" ...
If her eyes were open and if Andrea didn't...
Let her heart become cold while she gave in to temptation; succumbed to lust!

Smart girl, strong as hell, bad as can be...
Thought she could control outcomes, serve as more than a purpose, hold a place, on hold was her future for him; reserved; when all along what he planned to preserve, was his marriage protected by the walls of his home...

While what she deserved, she neglected, rejected, wrecked it, irreparable...
Until she deserved nothing more, Chris Bennett, no longer in it...

Small unit in which she now lives, walls enclosing or no?
Dealing with feelings or just letting go???
A woman, is made of body, mind, heart and soul...

Not perfect, especially when love is sought, the embodiment of so many things...

Often good, sometimes not...

Challenges we face! Where do we place ourselves, what are OUR goals, why do we attempt to insert ourselves into another woman's role???

We feel lost, lack of affection, abandoned, then suddenly affectionately smothered,
We feel heavily burdened and then suddenly we hover,
Because we believe we are "bad chics" floating as a result of a win, career or lover...

We sometimes find faults, create the figment of an enemy, and want to shove her,
Not realizing her image lays eyes upon us from the mirror...
In love, we are analytical creatures, protectors, magnetically drawn to highs and lows who so often suffer!

If I could teach I would teach the values, morals and attitude of Alice, the MOST beautiful mother...
Sometimes we get caught up in being our OWN, occasionally we can be selfish, greedy, snotty and then ten minutes later adorable, loving and needy.

We want it ALL! Respect! Love! A Man who lives to our standards! No second place feelings but top notch, touch the ceilings type feelings that make us feel high! We are demanding!

We are thoughtful but do not always think.
We are smart but do not always make intelligent decisions.
We are listeners who hear but so often refuse to listen...
We are women, these flaws make us real,
Embedded in us since birth,

Our ability to claim forgiveness but then nag you is
because we <u>can't</u>
                    forget;
                            it's a curse.

We are ladies, we are PRETTY, bad, Beautiful and worse.
We are scorned, we feel like something is owed to us,
therefore, we sometimes lose sight of boundaries,
We seek to play fair but sometimes forget the sport.
We call ourselves advocates, but success splits............us
apart.

We strive to be ladies and we NEED mothers like Alice to
teach us, warn us and (then) watch us fall,

We need those mothers who will pray, do, lift and threaten
to beat our butts at thirty...
Tell us "Yes sweetie, hell yeah you are worthy..."
But remind us to touch that which belongs to us and not to
long for man which does not......
To protect us from snakes and make sure that we do not
become one.

We are scorned! ....Scorned.....................
But we can break free from these heavy burdens, brush off
boulders from our shoulders, stop being angry at the man
who did us wrong, angry at the chic who has what we
want, angry at the player who in the game – won!

We can be better!
We claim ambition and when applied right it's the greatest
part of living! I believe in doing not wishing...
 "Doing" is the profoundness of a woman's ambition!

DOING allows us to do good, be good, create good, mold
good, be there when that good first becomes scorned,
save our children and all folks we meet like......

Alice, the MOST beautiful mother......

Enlightened by life, no feud, no wishing, no dissin,
spiritually sound, platinum edition, no greed -----

Her spirit is a gift to society.

October 8, 2014
#gottadobettah

"No Slammer"

Not a slammer but I couldn't resist
Being amongst this,
Talent
Opinion
Drive
Ambition
You know how us women....
do
Got so much to say,
Cause we over analyze.

I don't care if I get roasted or toasted,
Comedy at my expense is cool,
Your laughter, I'll host it...
Cause laughter is key to life,
One punch line
often creates a light...

When entering or trying to exit the struggle, there's gloom,
Unless your one of those witches able to hop a broom...
and leave
Whatever you do is better than attacking it with syrups or
shrooms....

Or any other narcotic....
Cause once you return from the erotic,
Mental state or sedate...
The gloom returns times ten...
See...
So being a woman...
of opinion
and ambition
Is all pretty,
Humility is key,
If I can laugh at me then I can be happy...

If you can laugh at me then cool,
Laughter is a tool....
Promising and pleasing to the spirit,
So, when you hear it...

Know that I'm steering you there,
Ride along with me.

August 2, 2015

SucCEEd
After
Your

Mistakes

"Of Loss"

Feeling it now, now that it has really hit home,
Fearing the future because it is positively unknown.

No fear shall exist, but the sadness lingers,
The thought of this and that creates such.

Misinterpretations of a bucket list for him and her,
Intrigued; embraced by both new and old; touched.

Forgiveness necessary? At one time or another it
becomes a need for each,
No worries about what to do when we look at unconditional
love and understand its reach.

Unconditional love empowers so much; so many are ready
to avoid; reluctant,
Do not fight the power of love; the pleasure of pain's
recovery; the dark that brings light; drops a hint.

2013

"The List"

I've let my hate for the hurt caused by you
To make me hate myself
It was my lack of self-priority, extreme tolerance
I realize now after God, I must be my #1 before I have "it"
to give to anyone else, makes sense.
I've let your manipulation, your constant displacement of
b l a m e
For your actions cause me to no longer love me...
I've let your deceptions – destroy – destruct
And break my spirit down
Destruct no more. Construct!!!!
My worth is as great as oceans and shores
I value me! My peace!
Soft as sand, calm as the Galveston Island Breeze
I deserve this and that; you've provided none of these...

I've been your concrete, your beams, your brick, your
plaster
I've built you up, meticulous design,
But somethings held you back...
Your many failures to move past her...
I've been your visionary, designer, developer, architect,
artist, agent,
Now that you're built...
I realize I'm gone, I wonder where my spirit went...

I've let the hurt caused by you...Shut me down...
Lifeless – existence in reality
Nothing --- not living just being
Existence – life – which is nice and all...
But it's not fulfilling
So I'm taking back those things I invested to make you
successful and appealing....
Smiles, Kisses, Writings, Encouragement, Coaching...
Preparation and seeing things through....
Abundance of so many things that were freely given to
you...

THE LIST!!!
I don't have to name them all...
You'll notice they've ceased in merely a short while

I talk a good game but will I really follow through????
Let's just say I'd be one hell of a bad chic if I did for me all
the things I've done for you...
But it's okay you see because deep, deep down...
inside, I still can...
I must focus now,
Press pass the small successes I've already achieved in
2013
Live life, seek serenity, cherish moments, feel internal glam
and...
Give thanks...

And, I start with you
Thank you for leaving me no choice
But to woman up and listen to my inner voice......

2013

"I Ask"

For any wrong I have done, I ask for your forgiveness.
I want to support you and your dreams; therefore, I ask for
your forgiveness.

For allowing my ambitions to shift; Causing one solely
shared goal to become two separate,

I ask for your forgiveness.

For forgetting the value of this "one" thing and for finding
flaws, I ask for your forgiveness.

For failing to see that my ambitions sometimes make me
flawed, for turning into Lauren from TLAM, I ask for your
forgiveness.

For being this Libra that demands balance and harmony
and pushes for such, I ask for your forgiveness.

For labeling "less thans" and striving for perfect, I ask for
your forgiveness.

For gathering data, creating lists and keeping points, I ask
for your forgiveness.

For not being vulnerable enough and blocking a true
intimacy from being shared, I ask for your forgiveness.

For sharp words, that nearly cut, for disrespect as
retaliation for "believed" neglect, I ask for your forgiveness.

For any right that was done for the wrong reason, for any
love misplaced, I ask for your forgiveness.

For any moment taken for granted, for any emotion
misguided, for any lack of terms of endearment, for any
fear sent, lost sight of what was meant,

to be
whilst not perfect…

I ask for your forgiveness.

September 23, 2014

"GRANDmother"

Bringing her back from Texas;
Getting her out of ish...
I can't imagine the worry she felt..,
when she'd ride the 18th all around.

Walking to Clarksdale...
from Preston,
Dying to get to 742 E. Jefferson;
to see Ms. Johnnie,

Walking to 316.....
East Chestnut to see...
him daily; glass in between,

Not realizing she had options beyond.

Barely is how much she knew KY or even the Ville,
Rarely to never, could she see any skin tone; only
requirement was friends must be "real"
Moving into Clarksdale; hanging in Shepherd
Square....see.....
Her heart found what she thought was beyond... (in
retrospect it was merely average love)
But she put it above...

And so,
y'all were so close,
You were wise and let her live a life she chose,
while thinking she was grown.
You knew she had a black eye behind those glasses worn
in no.....
sun,
But you protected her from a distance;
subtle teachings; your lessons didn't......
Go undone.
She didn't go untaught,
Senior year, a struggle but completion sought,

33

Damitrius a danger to her heart; like a blood clot.
Teenage love distraught.

After the first year, you could've made her move,
Instead you were judge free,
And grudge free; when she wasn't like you,
But your eyes only seen your "Pooh,"
smudge free.

You knew she'd change;
360 degrees,
Because of L-O-V-E...
LOVE of a life of adversity,
advocating diversity;
all parts of her personality,

She was intelligent....
creative, a writer,

A product of Galveston.....
Mind-shaping...

She doesn't know...
what happened.
You were her best friend,
Not just her grandma but her......
"Nanny" since her first words.
Suddenly, she's in her thirties,
And you all seem broken.
But please know she's been shaped by you,
Her love and respect is more than true.
Her admiration for "how you love" exists,
The love in her heart for YOU seeks and has NO exits...
She's encouraged...
and hopeful....,
because you and Papa shared deep love for one another,
Because of that, she knows God creates!
Miracles happen!
Life can be quick; finger snappin,

Support leads to joy and clappin,
Challenges are overcome,
Because of you, she knows breaking free from burdens
and hurtins,
is imper........ative,
She knows your love is declared,
And ongoing, it........is

Stating facts of life with.....without speaking,

"Showing..."

Unconditional love,

sometimes shaken,
never weakened,
NEVER taken.

February 16, 2015

"Way Full"

Nowhere near perfect mother
she's not even close
her worries stem from concern
her motherhood is her MOST
rewarding…Piece of who she is……
She loves her kids!!!

She is a mother not their friend
she's mean, she requires goals
She yells, is guilty of looking down her nose…
When grades are down
Gets mad when attitudes abound
gets fired up when their brains
are wired up…by wireless controllers and game…
systems

Making their minds incapable of independence
because games become the only priority
She's a mom who gets gritty
when angry about the things that aren't right
because she wants goals achieved
She envisions a certain life
for each of her three boys,
Her sons…
Who she loves so much…

She's a mother who makes mistakes, rushes and isn't
always playful
But her intentions are good and her heart is way full….
of love.

April 23, 2015

Cee

of

Love

"Mothers are Love"

Mothers are love because He told us to be
Mothers are tough but patient with a sense of urgency
Hardwired for survival; designed to respond to catastrophe,
Mothers are all things because He told us
to be
Formulated to keep systems running; updated accordingly
Making sure everyone has what they need...
"Mom I need a ride, I need some money"
And mothers "do" all of these "things" because that's what
He created us to do...

May 10, 2015

"Fought"

I have fought for you,
Fought against myself... Burdened my health, challenged
our wealth... Handled ish and dealt...
Fought off that which {appeared} to be greener grass,
pastures, rolling hills, freedoms.

I have fought for you...
Hated myself for allowing such, loss interest in you.....lived
dreams and nightmares, always wide-eyed waking back
up, shaken up, tangled in dried tears, rage and.......

I don't know how to cry, But I know how to fight, for you...
I don't know how to feel, But I know how to write about
you....I know how to be {right} about you and {wrong}.

I maintained...when you didn't, paved the way when you
couldn't, nagged and complained until YOU did IT...

Reconstructed walls that crumbled around me; laid floors
that you pulled out from under my feet. Designed ideas
and plans, while pretending to dance your beat...
While all along being the lady...

Who would bring you TO the best in you.........I left you no
option...but to...........because

I have fought for you...

More than I have for myself.....because my only choice, is
living as a "selfless" Libra, lyrically inclined, inspired to lift
others, "self-last..."

Twenty years, gone so fast...
Because I have fought for you...

Not for me...

I fought for you
because that is what
I am here to do,

I can preach a
thousand words......

about "lifting self"
and putting
self-first......

But my "self" includes you,
you include me.

You may be my hypocrisy...

But you are also my structure, Made of mostly...
Bricks thrown, mortar, scars stoned, feet dragging along, lit
by fire, burned by flames... ...but in the same...

You are the pyramid, the point, the high in me...
The "one moment anger" causing my self-absorbance, my
next minute cling; clung to you, holding on for life, in this
fight....Live or die, in its ugliest times...

Impeccable bond, cracked but unbreakable, fanned but un-
take-able, cold at times but un-fake-able...
Sparkling but sometimes lacking shine...

Smacked down but stacked back up, attempted hack but
firewall safe,

Built.
Challenged.
Yearly Struggles.

By some lame.... item thinking they are a "relative"
person...

We hurt and…
We…
Survive. Continue. Grow. Thrive.
In their eyes and thoughts.
But not in their sight…
……they can't cee us…
Because for you, I fight.

November 10, 2014

Love-
ExCEEdingly

43

"Round Two"

Pleasure, Desire! Pleasure, Desire! Pleasure, Desire!!
Can you feel it in your body – can you feel the desire
The heart's burning fire
Want!!! Not going to stop
Until it's achieved
Running around and round so busily
Pleasure pain!
Mistaken energy
Misunderstood vibes
Digging too deep
Insisting… to find what one seeks
Focused on what's wrong but not on what's right...
Determined; desire fulfilled
Ignoring the fact that all things come to light
All darkness becomes exposed
Body over mind, like whoa!!
Fail to think things through
Grasp the full extent
Success at accomplishing what's desired with you…
It's now real …. No longer just intent……
Pleasure pain pleasure pain pleasure pain, memories,
pleasure, pain, creating memories………which I'm happy
to gain
Intent of the heart; hidden some place
Simply tucked away, never locked, secured in its space…
Eager to become free, eager to be let lose, stray!!!
Straying—Not Staying – Emotions bundled up, pushed me
around…
Beat me up, kicked me when I was down
Now a woman scorned is a woman fed up………
Playing that song just twenty times more
Acting out what feels like a fairy tale
Following the lead of the body, ignoring the thoughts of the
mind, suppression suppressing all thoughts of the mind…
Mind control! Blown; Fully BLOWN!
Relaxed, more than content in this new zone.

Making brand new those things that were once ....part of
the past
It's been right since day one's first kiss
Round II, ooh I really missed that
So glad that you're here ...
To handle this...

February, 2013

"Along Came a Spider" aka "GSOC"

You are a spider,
Releasing your venom
Don't use the charm you have,
Don't turn it up on her...
Don't use that charm to
get all up and right in them....legs
unless you want her
tangled in your web,
Don't speak the words,
because they are your bite,
Don't sync with her
if you are not serious but
rather just a "maybe, I might."

Don't spark the intense,
Don't bite her on the neck

You are the outsider,
the spider that crept in from another nation,
She's the writer, longing to be lighter on the emotion, less
feeling –
While you come along, words you sling daily in your
dealings.

Along came a spider...while everyone is talking about
snakes.
Looking out for snakes, keeping the grass cut low,
You kept all eight legs hidden...
Charm, eyes, hands, face, voice, words, charisma, ability
to bring about her sin,

And then, delirious in her madness after the bite,
She gets her notebook and her pen, strokes it again and
again.................
back and forth with you – nothing making sense, eyes too
sensitive to see the damn light.

One moment she is intrigued, the next inspired, embodied, engulfed, embezzled by her own mind....cause she is capable but REFUSES TO SEE WHAT HAS COME TO LIGHT.

Looks in the mirror, turns to the side, two steps back, scaled back for two weeks...

Two weeks - now too damn weak. Giving in and giving out – the spider bit again,

You are worse than a snake, snakes just do it, out in the open and all...
You are a spider, carefully maneuvering your crawl.
Locking up so much of you, while using just the right parts of you --- to see her heart beat
your bite increases her blood pressure,
gets her racing a little and then..............
you watch her fall.

Oh spider, how dare you suck her in and have her cling to your web, stuck in all its dimensions,
All while expecting your name to never be mentioned,
Having her live in secret – not able to discuss your bite, creating tension,

She tried to get away, said she was done – but then you showed your power and she released all apprehensions...

It's your venom, your spell, the secretion you spit, the poison you secretly place when you bite her lip,

I said it's your venom, your spell, the secretion you spit, the poison you secretly place when you bite her lip

It's you, the GSOC, Great Strength of C; your own breed of spider and you know exactly who you are...

It's not that she is throwing a hint; it's that by that spider –
she's been bit.

Mammal. Woman. Mother. Strong…

But weakened by the nearly invisible spider – sneaky,
sultry, sexy, smart, seductive, scandal=us…

Chemistry kicking my ass and I have not even let down my
guard; this is only part of what could be us.

December 23, 2013

"I Want What I Had With You, With Him."

I want what I had with you with him.
The type of love you gave me,
His security, no risk, no danger...
Your kiss, your grasp, your breath-taking, awaking peace;
no anger,
But in my heart you are the rage,
For who, I wrote "lying to be your lion but not feeling
caged."
The one who took my flexibility beyond its original gauge,
The one who in my notebook is all the pages,
The one who I wanted to write about "not in chapters but in
stages."
It is that which has my mind outraged.........on the brink
of...it
with him..............

But your love...
          with that spider bite;

Venom sinks in.........
          my skin.................

I'm lost, on the outside looking in...
Thoughts of him are in my mind...........within......
What I know is right, but closed eyes see you again.

Eye lids wide open,
Focus lost, disturbed when you react to my words.......so
cost---------ly,
I toss......TURN......toss.........intensely...

Wonder where your hands might be wandering...
Start writing poetry......Look at my hand, see that ring

But owning up to the fact that he doesn't create that flow in me.

I want what I had with you with him…

Your lust; his loyalty……
Your bite; his arms each night
Your "bring about sin" ability; his stability
Your kiss; that heart of his…
Your thrilling; his willingness…

I want what I had with you with him.

March 30, 2014

"Weak Ties"

If you're the debt...
Then I 'm the ceiling...
Waiting for you...But without my
willing...
...ness,
Things between us accumulate, to mound a mess
I move higher and higher; extending...
For you I compromise....
Beyond what I should pretending...
Efforts what I should; pretending...
Efforts not wise; are these "real tries;"
Our bond is breakable, weak ties...
Our debts are forever realized.

April 2, 2014

"Feel Good Love"

These that you claim to be the softest you've ever felt,
If so, the gentle glide caressing you should
make…you…melt.

Resulting in you being in the palms of these,

Similar to how you are the topic of all of the.....
written and spoken word by me....

The softness that in the moment it seems......you live to
feel,
Gently fulfilling your demands,
Heart fulfilled, in its realest, most relevant.......
form of love, all happened by chance.

These hands....

Longing to enhance...that which you live and feel daily....
Because this heart provides blood to the fingers that write
about you, and rub you before and often after,
And provides the beat to the body of your greatest fan.

And these too? The ones you enjoy feeling as they....
Scribble scratch your back as you become inspiration for
new poetry...

Yeah... Across your creamy skin dancing... are these lips...
Freelancing.......words.......

While they move.......across your body while this mind is
zoned;
You know my stance....
My take on things...... well-rounded woman delivering.......

I WANT YOU; need you in my life.
So working these hands, lips, speaking through motions of
the tongue to plant....

That seed within you........

So that this is the woman you turn to...
When you need to rant; receive some reassurance,
When you need a "pick you up," a reminder that there IS
another chance...More opportunities, in this world for you.

It's these hands.....that touch you physically and this soul
which wishes to connect with your soul.

It's these lips that constantly talk; words flowing...

And it's these lips that kiss.....
every inch of you-knowing....
you deserve such feel good.
It's that feel good love and honor that comes with it...
It's those cherished moments...

These hands and lips-know you want it...

The softest you claim you've felt.
These lips and hands; the ones you vow get you so far
gone......it............

It's these hands...
That belong to the being who loves you more than oxygen
and land....

It's these lips that speak the words felt by the heart and
believed by the mind; saying "what we have is endless and
evolving like beach sands."

But most importantly between these hands and lips,
between this tongue that speaks and this pen that writes....

Is a heart that could never see you as a nuisance....
One that is in pursuance...

Established goals:

To have you choosing....
TO LIVE THIS LOVE OUT LOUD....
To give this love a deserving chance....

To feel, embrace the magical good and bad...
To live a life FULL of emotion...

Your daily routine inspired....
By that one great feeling of which nothing is better,

Two hearts together....
In love, in the deepest depths of devotion.

April 6, 2014

"Ironic"

I want to speak Spanish in your ear,
I want you to hear me before you feel me and feel me
before you hear me.

I want you to lift me and put me wherever you prefer,
I want you to grab me and take me back to that quaint, in
my mind, little place where we once "were."

Do what you want, when you want, manage this, kindle the
fire...
Because you are my great big desire!

I want to learn....

Because for you, I yearn,

By you, my life overturned,

By you, my heart burned,
Restless;
My mind still churns....

I yearn for you to be a force of good,
I long for you to do the things you've never done to me.

Cause you are my bad, my "wish I never had."
My remember that??? One helluva...

You are my temptation, my "no good can come of this."
My situation, my anticipation, my motivation,
My innovation in a world that was still; a life that was
settled; no battle,

But you being the player; the toy that you are; if you're the
baby then I'm the rattle...

Shaking me, you created me, this second Gwen....
My shadow now in...existence.....because....

You are my temptation!

You are the question to myself,
The timid wonder in my mind,
The skipped beat in my heart,
The blank page in my notebook,
When writing about you just isn't "enough."

You are the ink in my pen; flowing....
when I wish not...
You are my controlling...
You are temptation I never asked for but got.

You are my eyelids when they close at night,
You are the arms of my chair as they wrap me as I sit at
my desk...
I work hard for you because you've caressed......
Internally and externally....
Every part of me.
You are my temptation, my devil, my fall, my "I'm sorry,"
my "My, My, My" and my "Why, Why, Why."

You are this thing which is great......and massive,
From which I've tried to escape....
You are my highs and lows...
my aggressive and my passive...
I remain engulfed!!!...not free.
Drowning in the gulf that is you,

One day calm waves, sailing at sea,
The next, throwing salt....
Of all the fish, REALLY? I'm the one you caught.
Now I'm caught up; sensible thoughts chucked...

"In love with temptation."

You are my devil, my spider; your poison my
sickness....My weakness....
My "I need you to take me."

My ironic; my narcotic.....

Addicted as a result of trying to recover from your venom,
my "please boy don't fake"....see?

You are my "knowledge" in my world from which you've
stripped all logic.

June 25, 2014

"And Then You Sweat"

Keep telling yourself not to do {or say} anything you will regret...
And......then......you......sweat.
Eyes closed, heart stopped ....breath lost......

Heart no longer needs to race, you stop EVERYTHING for that embrace......
And......then...you......sweat............
Him again, mind wondering, if your mind ever speaks what its thinking 99 percent of the time...

Are you prepared for your warranted loss?

"Gem-in-eye"

Sex as a weapon
His alma mater she's reppin
His shirt...........................Caresses her skin
Reminiscing.............................Of him
Knowing his evil twin....................Is lurkin,
Soft spoken, innocent she
Loudly chosen, spicy, curry
Signs of astrology....................not properly
Warned.............................Prophecy
Ripped she is, torn.
Confused by his darkness and his light, two shades,
Wonderful and catastrophic
Endearing and daring; the dominate gentleman
Forcing in and out of zones
Taking her to galaxies
But smashing like a blackberry......Storm... in 2k8; she's
always kept him fed; made sure he ate.
Once embedded as a core.................................in his
palm...
Pilot no flame
No fire........................But threatened by heat
Feel the wrath of the......
Cold-hearted..........................Unwilling to finish what's
started
Closed book, guarded...
Sex as a weapon....................His sword.
Bound by....................................the evil Gemini,
Her "gem-in-eye"
Vision impacted....................Image
flawed..................And yet all
She does is spit on his mic
He acts it, she writes
Influential...................................Affair
In her mental...
With him is where
she is.........
Not broken but repaired

Mended...

Mutual consent............

to end it.........

Inevitably weak...
juices flowing like wet ink...

Sex, the weapon.................Sensual seek,
New "piece" coming; Poetry sneak
Her "gem-in-eye" too deep....
Shabby, shallow embraces,
Yet, hardcore thrusts...
Intertwined mingling fingers, touching lace
Saving face; filling spaces,
Penetrating perfectly designed places...

Real performances so fake

She takes.......................

The token, Gemini.

May 6, 2015

"Render Myself Back to Me"

I want my closure; please don't make me beg
I've recovered for the most part
from your poison, that venom, that sickness that struck me
Causing my blood to race, enlarged heart

Near death
I lived on the edge, Trying to please you
Broke every set of rules I placed in my life; disposed of my own ethics;

Misplaced my morals
because the feelings you delivered I had never fathomed...
The emotions you enabled, yes those you openly
encouraged yet secretly
discouraged...

Made all...things....right
The weighing down, did he or not,

The self-inflicted trauma the endless love sought drama...
All ceased in your presence
because you made all things right

For you I went from me to an upgraded version
I was even more impressive until....

No....no.....let's just stop!

No long drawn out poetry piece this time!
Especially when an entire CD has already been the result
Thank God for my ability to revolt
Though not easy, I'm better

I've accepted the scars, the tarnish I shall forever wear;
that hue that will faintly................be present

I ask for my closure; it is needed from you, I demand it
Please give it to me.

I need my calm; the "normal" world I once knew to return

You're no longer invited so you need...
to render myself back to me
because I need my closure

It's not yours to keep, you see....

May 31, 2015

"Autopcee"

Why did you choose more than external?
And decide to bring to the outside what is meant to be
internal.............................ized?
Your lies...
Is it because it's a way of forgiveness.........
for your secrets witnessed
only in dark and not in light?

What did you find as you dissected me?
What have you learned as you got brain from me?????
What knowledge did I drop on you? Enough to make you
drip?

What did you feel as my heart beat
once synched
with the muscle in your chest stopped?
Did you feel a pause?
Did you find proof of cardiac arrest?
Or just trauma...
Arteries clogged by the fog...
Induced drama
you created to keep me confused
So that I could never truly love you, because you would hit
to merely leave bruised.

What did you see when you opened me?
When you inflicted uneasiness through a line drawn by
your tongue across my torso?
Did you not see the rib graciously accepted?
Or was it that you more so
loved yourself over all other beings...
both cherished and neglected?

Tell me what it is that you now see...
As you pull my eyelids back, open wide,
Soft brown color, gentle even in death
As you caress my hair..........to the side and stare

Do you see the Angel that I was or the Ghost...that...I have...become?
As you press my fingers in ink,
To confirm that it's me,
Do you read between the lines of my pointer now getting the point?
Do you take from my ring finger a treasure that you now wish to treasure?
As you pry apart lips that use to refrain from too many explicits as a result of pain,
Do you see the tongue that use to cut?
Do you see fear of the death of us?
As you remove my parts with your hands,
Do you find proof of life, "evidence?"
That we once were so much in love, love making heavily dense...

Continue to examine...
As you autopsy me ---
Cut me gently with precision,
Shine light on what's been hidden,
Observe my beauty neglected,
Uncover all the tragedy – sickness, infected...
Why are you rummaging inside of me? What do you wish to retrieve?
Is it your heart you rendered mistakenly?

June 9, 2015

"Angry Woman ---- Got'Em"

Angry Woman...
Has she reached her highest impact capacity?
She says no, but his false
Sword keeps
penetrating her... repeatedly.
His foul play - a variation of control, sob stories, light
filtering as he sucks the brightness to dark
Developing an imminent danger, of being stranded, battery
dead and bitchiness as he rides her then parks
She feels penned to paper, she feels only as bold as her
ink, apparently
She's clipped ---- when she wants to be the staple.
She's no dip stick --- she just found his stick able
To maneuver barren roads,
that had never been ....exposed,
creating mental pits stops along the way, heartbreak hotel,
hell's kitchen; café; dicing breasts as if he would consume
her, too many to name...
Instead she consumes him again
As all she wants is to be...
The permanent connector of his world and his destiny
The driveshaft, the controller of what happens while she's
in drive, fueling up to thrive
But she merely continues to exist... idle, damn near
powerless.
Her eyes bright, headlights on high beam
in those moments of "auto start, no smoke but
steamed......windows, passion on the hood,
the control; just a thumb, a simple press to open ...up
Nothing in life is ever as good
as being care free with your arms steering see

Her eyes then cut, dropping low, salt water flows as her
head gasket blows,
Her shoulders shift, her hands fist and the gear switches
Then feeling a drag, she clenches and wishes she did not
get in his groove,

She attempts to move, back-arched
and mouth set to yell like a car alarm – secure in its "look
but don't touch me" mode ready to ward off dramatic
scenes and to reward unparalleled parking because...
She should NEVER be behind you while you are looking
forward.
She's pissed!!.... That she gave you pole position when
you never qualified
That your track record proved flawless at being fraudulent
That you can convince truth that it is a lie...
You won, take your victory lap, reign in it and reap your
benefits
She retires from competition,
Takes the lap of honor
PS: Check your brake lines and yo lug nuts...
you have none left.........
Got'eeeeemmm

June 11, 2015

Let Me CEE You Write

"I Write"

I write because no one listens when I speak.

"It's because no one wants to hear the truth that's told by you."

I'm sure many - understand the way in which this goes,

You speak, scream, shout...
but you might as well have just whispered to your soul.

I write because no one listens when I speak.
"Clearly."

I'll share a story now but I know it shouldn't leak,
"Dearly."

June: fun for most; hot; happiness from sunshine,
But once love existed; before; now past; left behind.

If you can follow, then you've clearly shared a loss,
Unexpected, realized he was no longer there; such a shock.

I write because no one listens when I speak.

Strangely though, others want to know me; touch my leg and say "so smooth..."

I share simple sarcasms; single remarks; always contemplating my next move.

I write because no one listens when I speak.

I share words written in ink; typed in docs
or posted on a wall,

Which go ignored but I feel different; complete.

Oddly enough, they're read in full after the phone rings; oh, that dreaded call.

I write because no one listens when I speak.

June 2013

"My Notebook" a.k.a. "All She Wrote"

My notebook knows my thoughts;
It got to know me to well too quick…

Gently, I write my words,

using a plain bic…

Allowing it…

to know what makes me tic...

Days later,
I look back and give myself a kick,
It pays attention to all; thinking it's slick.

It understands the messages hidden between the lines,
Takes my hints; helps me live,
encourages me to remove my disguise.

It has me bound, spiraled up
Shiny, lying on one side

It knows I'm trying to change the game….

"Hmmm, should I show some
love to Rupp?"

My notebook keeps me neat and organized; prioritized…
I fold the corners down, rub the page gently and then……

I stroke the pen……

It records my goals, Responds to my needs…

Little does it know, the lines aren't blurred;
My vision is clear: I write my thoughts, indeed.
I listen to what my notebook says,

It tugs at me; Says "Yeah," and tells me to "be patient and enjoy the ride.

Therefore, on its words I put a spin......
It understands the feel'in......

Then I refrain from acting on impulse,

My notebook cares; protects...
Is intelligent; at its utmost.....
Positive, and all things I expect.

My notebook loves my ink,

When it goes on wet......
When I let....................it help me relax,
When I'm above it, on my elbows I rest,
When I'm riding, I mean writing......It knows I'm no threat.

It was my desire to open him up; See its clean and bare pages;
Apply my touch, Learn about his insides, write a story - not in chapters but
in stages...

I want to fill him up so he is no longer blank...

Awaken him...
be what tickles him; be the feather on the pen that glides over
him.

My notebook is entertaining; Daily new discoveries,
Sometimes difficult to comprehend; But inspiration he's bringing...

He delivers; Thanks to the greatness he gets from his Mother.

He gets a little bold like a Sharpie;
accepts me in all my moods, every color...

Would let me write thousands of recipes in him...
Because he loves food, and reads me as his menu.

Sometimes I want to glue something on him,

Then I realize there's no reason to cling,

Instead I hold him close; he's big and blue and doesn't fit in my purse...

But I carry him because he protects my spoken and written words.

Sometimes I want to wad him up,

Sometimes I want to flatten him out and
pencil all over him...

Scribble-Scratch his back;

Massage him with a twirl of my tongue,
He loves my silent words;
I love speaking through my tongue on his skin.

Sometimes I want to take a page and place it in a bottle,

Message sent; Floating: Someday to be found and read...
All while, I remain here with my notebook going full throttle.

Sometimes I want to remove all of his pages...

And see only his skin; at others I want to shred him...
Into tiny pieces...

So that I can achieve puzzling him to back to whole...

I love my notebook and all that he shows...
That he represents all things that he knows...
The thoughts of mine, he holds...

The fact that he's always willing to chill with me and see
how my story   unfolds............

I want to be who he is speaking of when he
says...............

"That's All She Wrote."

November 3, 2013

You Can't CEE Me

"You're the City"

I don't owe you contrary to your popular belief
You're the city – I'm the one who never sleeps
You're the city – big time you—

      Trying to be a metropolis
I'm suffering – tired of being taxed by you
      Ready for the street to clear so I can get past this

Ready for the traffic light to permanently turn to red
Ready for your inconsideration to result in not one tear
shed…
Shed, storage, you're the city
Big time you; I'm on leased space
However, not indebted to you; challenged; denied

My mind burdened by images of your face
Pace; speed, keeping up with others
Facebook, twitter, email, text…

You are social media, you are that article in the paper, and
you are the city

Relentless, in your ways, with crevices, hidden alley
images that do not often surface…
Boxes, tape, packing,
I must move; relocation in order to seek my life's NEXT…

Bit of charm…
Charmed life guaranteed,
Life free of pity……………….
As I choose to leave.

Leave… live free, live worry free
Live simple days,
While you hustle and bustle, city lights, grinding your life
away; many ways
Ways – acts- threats- things that will change you

As my lack of residency begins to take its toll, its cost…
Your loss!!!!!!!!!!!!

Broken bricks, cracked sidewalks, shattered windows,
graffiti benches
Art it might be – but you don't know
Since you are a city – only concerned with your OOWWNN
growth
Not open to culture
Believing all others are irrelevant
Dismissing opinions, consistently lacking the ability to
care…
Leaving my only choice to move, I no longer live there.

Saying to others, "I used to love……
"Now it's just a city where I once went"
You're the city big time you ---
Failed to give back to the spirits- now in tragedy or disaster
will you get through????

February 2, 2013

"Too Weak to Let the Wrong One Go"

Too weak to let the wrong one go.
You claim to be so strong,
You motivate others to make moves,
When it comes to yourself – heart's been leading too long.
Your stuck in a rut; grinding; daily groove.
Too weak to let the wrong one go.
Used to be so smart; dedicated; ready for the world,
Still are; sticking around to do what's right; now hidden;
now bored,
Down for whatever, adventurous, intelligent, cute and good
girl,
Lack of appreciation; he's failed you; no longer ignoring
that your person has been ignored.
Too weak to let the wrong one go.
Ignored? In all forms – written and verbal too,
Ignorant? He but not me; never,
Important? A little, I guess,
Backup plan? Savings, soul, strength stashed; I am still
clever.
Too weak to let the wrong one go.
So tired, don't know what I'm think'n,
Us right'chea – days of the old attraction,
Too weak to let the wrong one go; against my mind; sink'n,

Too much discrepancy, disappointment, discouraging
distraction.
Making me feel like I'm less, a fraction,
No not quite; don't think you will get away with that so
easy,
I am whole, an important being, soldier girl, geometry,
Drop the "e" see "go-me-try" to do good for me and that is
good-bye.
Too weak to let the wrong one go?

Secrets, deception,
Manipulating angles,

Your actions lack all that is true,

Points don't connect,
Nor did they ever…

Tired of working
alone for a configuration;
I drew the line, obsolete,
the pair is not there,

Magician or mathematician,

Either way; no two way relationship with you,

As I stand alone; I seek my own transformation.
What will it be or what person will exist?
That answer is not yet; may never be known,

But internally SHE will be prized, top-notch bisch, number
one and queen of the throne.
Too weak to let the wrong one go?
No!

Spring, 2013

"Crack the Lens"

It scares the hell out of me, that I am no longer afraid of the permanent loss of you…
That I no longer choose to suffer…with you……………
But rather I could see our envisioned permanence come to an end.
It surprises me that I am finally able to seek happiness without the fear that always crept up,
The thought of happiness is tugging harder and harder at me; no longer wishing to withstand being fed up...

I always wished and waited and therefore, withstood the negatives, waiting for the positive to develop…
The thoughts I now have, the motivation I feel, the words that come from my mouth, showing that some of 2k12 and 13's thoughts are not just intense but real…

The thoughts of doing this or that and not wondering if I could ever get back…
to you…

The words from another who said "damn, you really don't love him anymore." The shock that it brought to that person with the realization of such…
See, we were often the strength for the group, the encouragement for the two who might be on a fence, pondering their next move…

Everyone knew it was never perfect but everyone lived vicariously through us in some way and thought that to each of us "it" would always be worth it.
Worth the worry, anxiety, sad time and sacrificing of so much,
Well, I am no longer afraid to tell others not to sacrifice themselves; rather seek what delivers the touch…
The touch on your heart; that little urge that you feel…
That one thing that makes you speechless and you aren't

able to explain; the tiniest impact that makes you happy, with no act...

That is precisely the result of a positive impact!!!
Love your "you!"
If you do not have it to give to yourself; then you def don't have it to give to anyone else.
Karma creates this cycle, yeah, later you get to take your "get even" shot...
But the best way is to just drop the camera, crack the lens, walk away and brush your shoulders off.

November 11, 2013

"Smart Chic"

So, let me make sure I got this right…
You don't want to be hated, you say…
Then why blur that thin line between love and hate?
Why walk on it, wobbling from side to side,
Failing to strike real balance.
All it takes is "Just being honest."
Like future sees the past… you lied.

Poor her,
I can't imagine what she put up with,
In and out, face here and there,
Arrested not developed,

Photos…
Oops, I mean mug shots,
Wanted, hot,
Not willing to stop,

Sought by several counties' cops.

Let's blame it on a possible gambling problem
Or you unwillingness to express yourself, hidden behind
walls built of rays, no one allowed to dissolve them.

Just fake!

Tiny bit of you; even tinier is the amount of anything true!

On for the take; for what you can; when you can;
seemingly stuck between "man" and "grown man."

Hiding behind an image polished to a tee,
Perfectly presented in the eyes of Gwen Cee; now her
dilemma…

Been sitting on this piece for about two months, knew it
was coming

Damn, it is something…

Why does the smart chic chase the dumb di@#?
Or why did she?

How do we suppose that happens?

Game changing, notebook paper, scribble scratched by the
tongue, words spit and then spider bit, not just a one and
done, constantly fighting the battle, seeking resolution!

Damn, why would a smart chic chase the dumb d1@%
and allow herself under such influence?

Answer to be determined; as I always say I'm not judgin…

Rather, I'm hidden like I'm the forbidden,
My words removed as soon as seen when written,
that dumb di@% unable to handle a woman who is
driven…

February 24, 2014

"Unwanted"

No one wants anything,
No one needs any of that.
No one is in competition with you (nor have they ever been)...
It does not matter who was first or second or middle or last,
It does not matter who is the boy or who is the girl...
None of that matters.
Your frustration leaks from an internal dismay,
Your unhappiness is from within so maybe, someday - you may...
Become that adult, a mature woman so you will no longer need to pretend...
Sadly mistaken the words you have written in the past,
Your mind boggled in its own disturbing cycle, we all thought would pass.
Keep in mind and hear me loud...
No one wants or needs anything that you continuously compete about.
Amazingly those "no ones" who I speak of have been treated as such...
By a select few while they desired to be dear, but "they" are so loved...
So loved, so loved by them, so loved by us...
Kind, giving, sensitive, mature, dedicated, loyal "men!"
But you?
Blind, taking, uncompassionate, pain in the a$$,
royal...rotten!

2014

" Rant-Uh-Tree "

If someone did that for you...
Put themselves second in an attempt to achieve ... all
things that are YOU

To help you find who you are meant to be...
If someone did that and achieved,
Successfully......making you more than what you
previously dreamed.

If someone did that; helping you make means,
Assisting in the startups of what you hoped for...
Partnering in your growth on a level you've never seen
before...

If someone did that season after season, struggle after
struggle for sixteen years of time...
Who are you to vaguely misrepresent that bond in the
sixteenth?

Then to continue on, only claiming this and that and then
reaching the nineteenth...
If someone did these things that YOU couldn't have done
alone,
Who are you to ignore all things that have been done for
you?
Does ignoring those efforts and accomplishments of
"someone" mean you are ignoring YOU?
Staying true to YOU requires staying true to...
someone.

September 29, 2014

"No Handles"

Run your courts...
Enjoy your fame....
Go hard...in... the...paint!
At least you're going hard at something,
Ambition was never your strongest attribute,
But you've always thrived when the focus is on you.

You like the center position
Or being the center of attention
You've been troubled by rebounds
Never heard the crowd's cheering sound.
So it's visible....
That you think your dream is livable
Who knows? Maybe.
But points count in life
Who's counting though?
One of your fav------orites
That phrase is......
"There's no I in team"
Well there's no I in us,
There's too many loss opps, too many missed shots
Too many "forgots"
Just too many losses....
Too hard to deal with.

Organization has basically failed,
Because of lack of respect and turnovers to the opponent,
When they went for the ball,
Harder than who "should've" been included.
Not sure if it's point shaving...
But actions speak louder than all sayings,
When your team gets fed up...
Feels the need to contact the rival,
breaking loyal,
You should ask yourself "what led up?"
----to this...
Should have paid attention...

To the suspensions,
maybe should've been fined,
So the interest in the commentators and sidelines
wouldn't be your team member's newest find.

Sad for you,
The dynamic duo, only takes two!
And, all rewards which comes with such
Right in your hands but you lost your dribble
YOU should've learned to go "right!"
You needed handles,
You focused on points and popularity,
Not wins and clarity!

Basketball didn't get married!

June 3, 2015

Truth
CEE'rum

"Set Up"

See, it was set up,
That she became fed up,
It was cause he wouldn't let up...
Crazy; running around the "screets,"
Talking bout "bet that,"
      "That's my cat..."
          "You go'n do me like that?"
Completely unmotivated on working; so instead of...
He was planning a "come up,"
Some sort of scheme; a quick get up...
To increase his net...up,
But "For What???"
A few dollars,
And, so his life would've...
    Had the threat of....
   ...."ending."
(See the point to where this poem led up?)

February 15, 2015

"Baby Man"

So, I seen a post
Someone was glad for the snow
Said it would keep someone from being dead
But that's not true cause two weeks prior when the snow
fell
So did you.

The same folks who gave us
Guns
Are the same ones who picked P to sell our youth to be
soldiers
And to have no limit
I'm in love with Tupac, that I won't deny
But I'm not raising my three boys to see things only
through his eyes
But I encourage them to listen to certain words and
remember when he said "be the mind."

Well…that's what I tell them
"Be the mind"
To change yourself
The world
Or spark the mind who will
Because
One in three end up In jail
One possibly resting…in peace
And baby like so many………
Mothers…
all I have is you three.
I need you to live
Let others do the same
Don't get caught in this "game"
Cause this game isn't on a board
Or played with a deck
It's…
on soil and you can be above or six feet below it…
Baby

Become! JUST BECOME...
A kid, a teen, a dreamer, an adult, a goal and a leader...

Make your own examples and embrace......
life, don't disgrace......
yours...
and never......
take one...
Man.

March 4, 2015

"Question"

Mug shot versus prom picture face
Media's choice to display, media's disgrace.

I'm outraged...

This is my outcry.
because kids are getting killed outside.....

And, the role of the media's hype, it's blaze is to outline a
certain race,
To negatively reinforce a tainted image, yet positively
endorse those who deserve blemish.

Why is Social Security monetarily lined up for him?
But Social Security in the form of bars for them?
Is it because he wears khakis and a polo and he's quote
"disturbed?"

Let's see how it would be if a black man, 42 asked your
kids to come inside
If he tried to entice...

Would he still be disturbed or "not all there?"

And Mr. Officer, do you think it's right when
you give me feedback of your conversation with him
and you tell me that he was bawling his fist up at you...
Let a black man do that shit...
and the worry we have for our kids
would've been through...
Cause you would've nipped that in the bud, right on the
spot
but
because he's a white man
42, gray hair, khakis, a polo, no Jordan shoes......
all we got

was a response
from you……
that he's not…
"all there"

and we shouldn't feel threatened...

Question:

His fist, his aggression?!?!
No need to pull your weapon???

April 21, 2015

"Nervous System"

The row of connected bones down the middle of the back
the back that carries the burden of life
for most, the need for food, water shelter, love and
affection
but for some the need for acceptance
or at least a fair contest
just based on skin or tone or culture or face or being
viewed as mattering less
SPINE!
Vertebrae…support of body…LIFE!
That shall be allowed as would any other
he's a son, he's a brother, he's a father
can't imagine the pain endured by many mothers…
SPINE!   Protecting the spinal cord…
"connecting all parts of the body to the brain"
never, should it be severed
by any, especially those…
who are supposed
to uphold
protect and serve us
SPINAL CORD AND BRAIN = CENTRAL NERVOUS……..
System designed for human life
When did living daily life in America literally become a
"NERVOUS SYSTEM?"

April 21, 2015

Short Poems by Gwen Cee

Definitely protest! Please.
What are they doing?
Minds lost, lives ruined, God help.

April 21, 2015

Standardized statistics sick
Enough to evolve,
From alarmed to awake.

April 21, 2015

"No Good Cause"

I love it when we make excuses for co—opss
Who profile folks as society's knock-offs
Who harm people when they let shots off?
For no apparent reason...
"Accidental, heat of the moment,
Was "concerned,"
So much that the only answer was to completely end a life

"The only detainment
was to contain him
under the barrel of my gun"

Or maybe we make excuses
For so many reasons that a reasonable person will never
understand
A "reasonable" member of society

No officer,
You are trained to be sound, not to flash your weapon
around, not to fire for no good cause
Not to harm those who needed safety, which is why you
were called.

Terribly, you don't even know that the good officers, the
cops...
who honor the badge, protect, serve and do their "jobs"
Carry the burden of your actions
Your infractions that may seem small to you
Give no peace to family sizes that have decreased
Based on your part in declaring the deceased
And result in no good light on officers across the states
Because although, there are likely many who wish to
uphold, your actions change the state...

You create a reason for "why is this happening" "how is
this possible" "what can we do"

You bring burden to people who create funds for a salary for you
While you are toting your gun, which this time was not used
How would you feel if you were told not to speak with a gun pointed at you?
Better yet, where is your child,
Does she have a bathing suit?
Yeah, how would you feel?

Your emotional level has nothing to do with the response you should make
Your emotional intelligence should come into play

Do right behind your badge, protect it, what happens in sleeping hours comes out in full power the next morning.

June 11, 2015

"Nothing Left"

Street peddlers WILL and CAN sell anything
It's their way of life
Sparked minds and dedicated hands
Find the knock off of any item you've ever wanted in
Manhattan.
Once in Queens, "Frogs $5, 3 in a case, get them all today
for 12; it's good."
And, in Tribeca, the sidewalk structures and smell is an art;
Vibrant to us; to them a...LIVELIHOOD...

I've walked Flatbush and the Colosseum of

Jamaica Queens

And the hussssstle is

everything...

The hustle

is far more than

the eyes can
see
It's a reality,
a grind,
Like so many others couldn't know, wouldn't know and
shouldn't know
It's the result of a G.D.A. – "Government Designed and
Approved" system
Used to categorize and imprison minds
Which could do anything

But to allow that "truly" equal opportunity would be insane
For the control mechanisms of America would shatter
The white man would no longer be the mechanic of our
society.

The inks of picturesque stories folks tell their children
would splatter
With truth --- that no one wants to hear
With weight
With I's dotted and t's crossed with perfection
Because the brains they tried to keep in sections
Like the old Cabrini Greens, The Wards, even our own
Clarksdale and Sheppard Square,
The brains in physiques of bodies need to be freed
To become encouraged minds, no longer labeled or
identified as an outcast of a society
Which they help build and culturize...

But fear of a creativity, fear of a culture exists by those who
continue to profit...
from the lock downs, the courts' stock up and now the
shock of what "we" allow.

People, who "look" like me... What we allow and what we
do and...
What we see every day and we turn the cheek the other
way
Making us need to {SMACK} ourselves
WAKE THE HELL UP!
People.
        America.
                Nation.

If you claim difficulty in your past and you claim goals and
planned impact,

"YOUR MARK ON SOCIETY"

Then the only way to make that impact is to
unite the nation
take part in nothing that divides races
Give up the verbatim...
Bullshit you have been taught and are teaching.

You have no other option…

You either do this and LOVE ALL OTHERS or we are all going to fall…

A nation of which there is "nothing less" than

Because we will have nothing left…man.

July 26, 2015

Hear No Evil;

Cee No Evil

"Not Your Princess"

I used to get a high off people looking at me...
I wanted to be interesting,
Outgoing, have many friends, But somehow... through the
years I've let you break me down,
There is not a peep left in me, not a whisper, not a sound,
my confidence is nowhere to be found...

But I'm here to tell you NOW, that you know, it's okay to
expect a lot from the person you love...
I love my "me," average, not perfection -- While you make
unfair comparisons...

I'm not your Tiye, if you want me to be then I'll have to say
see ya;
I'm not your Lisa if you think I am then I'm going to have
say I'll miss ya
I don't have the confidence of your Tammy; instead my
nerves get going and my palms get clammy
I'm not your Sherry but if you want me to be; I'll saaayyy...
your life might be scary
Scary because I'm none of those girls from your past but if
you keep comparing me, then I might become just that...

I'm a grown woman with children, real estate, degrees and
responsibilities...
While you compare me to those memories and images
from when you were young – but see... those were little
girls...
I'm not a little girl......AND... "I'm not your princess, I'm
your
wife"

My hair gets frizzy; not always straight and smooth,
But I'll keep you straight; as I chose to leave Houston and
launch a life with you.
I'm not your princess; I'm your wife,
My eyes are brown; no special color,

When your vision is put to the test; I'm your sight,
Helping you achieve your mission; one way or another.

I'm not your princess; I'm your wife!!!

My complexion isn't perfect; no whitened smile here,
Plenty of smiles I share with you; open mind; helping you
navigate as you steer.
My nails aren't always polished; plain, clear
But my hands...are caring; arms want to hold you, if I were
in another galaxy... I'd find a way to get near...... you
I'm not your princess; I'm your wife...
I'm not 5'8, actually lucky to be 5'2,
Legs short, pretty feet, gravity pulls me to where you are...
Sort of cute; spontaneous; smart,
If I built ...the ship ...you'd be the captain...
Loyal, I am! I'm there when you rise... and... when you
descend.

I'm not your princess; I'm your wife,
My shoulders... are broad; my tan... often barely... shows,
skin soft...
I help carry your burden, those things that weigh on your
shoulders, I lift and take them; I blast!!! them off...

I'm not your princess; I'm your wife,
Not perfect like the stars in the night sky,
Strangely though, others want to get to know me...touch
my leg...and say "so smooth".........
I share simple sarcasms as defense mechanisms to hide
the painful truths...
Even if I love you from the Earth to the Sun to the Moon,
The greatest space I share with you is my heart and the
greatest gift is that which came from my womb.
I'm not your princess... I'm your wife...
I can be difficult, I'm not your joyride,
Rather, I'm your lifelong endeavor...
I'm more than an exploration, supporting you in adversity,

I keep your secrets, give you clearance and bring you pleasure...
As the sounds of the Earth become a whisper; as the lights become a faint glimmer...
You will always be my saint even as we depart this world where sin occurs......
Whether we remain in this one or travel to another dimension...
My love for you remains undeniable; for my love for you brings no apprehension.
Wherever we go, when we get there......then......
I will be your princess.
But right now on this planet, on Earth,
I'm not your Princess, I'm your Wife.

Revised Summer 2013

"Falsehood"

I will pay,
For twenty years of my life and,
That is to Sallie Mae,
Or Uncle Sam...

Before getting it through dropping of a skirt or pants,

Because
my mind is strong and leads; I do not need...
To schedule a date with chance.

I am a woman, driven, clearly vocal and full of rants,
intelligent,
No need to use the softness of my skin,
I will make it
because my mind is...capable...

I do not use my body,
I do not use my sensuality,
As a force...
And, no matter how badly,
I want IT, I refuse to lean that way for recourse,
I refuse regret or remorse...

If every single piece of me desires it, I take action!
Knowing when He says, it shall happen,
As a result of my ambition not from sitting on his lap and...

Well...

I AM going to get there,
I am already steps ahead,
I will continue to pray for those who make us all look
unfavorable
Those who lack integrity,
Those who climb the wrong thing,
And claim,

The wrong fame…

I will continue to be a professional,

Doing the right thing; so everyone knows…

My career I own,

I built it!
My internal power, I wield it.

I shall not hold a grudge,
Against a woman who climbed up,
And plucked the apple from the tree.

She chose to use hers differently,
While I remain on bended knee.

Praying for protection and guidance,

To help me to not despise…
What is not fair…

To encourage me to realize,
Without her way she would have never gotten there.

She is weak-minded, clearly not weak-kneed,

I must not worry,
About her and her toxicity.

I am rational, reasonable and well advised; resourceful and sound.
Her ONLY way to the top was to lay down.

I'll pray for her too,

Because a woman who will do,

Anything to get anywhere,
Has NO control over her life,

If she cannot create her own real world; successful in its
right,
Then someday she will be exposed,

At that moment she will not be material for a lady, Leader,
Friend or Wife,

As in that moment the falsehood of the woman she
portrayed will show.

April 2, 2015

"Two Feet In"

It's sad not knowing where you stand with someone,
Consistently asking yourself without even knowing,
Is this ground solid, soft, ready to crumble or covering a
quake?

But it's worse when you have to wonder why you don't
know where you stand,
"Did I do something, was it always a game, is the player
not real but fake?"

In times when stress or worry often block happiness and
burdens carefree spirits,
In times of a gloom, a darkness across society,
Disappointment and anxiety,
Knowing the truest form of love,
the softness and kindness of love is critical

In times when we are all so connected to the entire world
through devices,
But our love is shown on pages and not in hands
In these times we need to show one another where they
stand, what place they hold in our lives, what beauty they
bring to our worlds...

So...

Life is too short for one foot in and one foot out,
Give your family, children and friends all of you,
Or your failure to be involved and responsive creates a
mental gap,
Leading to....
a broken confidence, burdens preventing hap------
iness
Or wasted time considering
"Am I good enough?"
"Is this dynamic a healthy one?"

If you're leaving people to wonder........
then likely you're...
not doing your best,
you're doing no one any favors
nor contributing to creating a better world...

See, there was a time when...
it seemed, I could do no wrong...

Back then...

Suddenly, when I was no longer "Perfect....
Patty,"
There was no sudden quest....
Or question of "what if?"
No instantaneous epiphany...
Instead a conscious decision that I had to "do better"
Which resulted in changes, within self, internally
But I didn't change those around me,
Because they were already in with two feet,
Not one.
I respect them for that,
I made improvements so in return I could better love back.

May 10, 2015

"Ingrained Interpretation"

Supported all these folks and places
I can take my skin off, maybe be as fleshless
As I am selfless.

The skin, it's not mine
I'm just in it, it keeps cartilage intact to allow me to grasp a
pen...
It's borrowed, it houses what creates thoughts and brings
ideas to life.

In my flesh you will find a person.
In my mind and spirit, you will witness a poet.
I have ideas that matter whether I show it

I write words
Words I recite
to allow folks to develop their own interpretation
Hoping to ignite
Something inside of someone
To allow their benefit
As a result of my form of art

I don't need
to convince you to believe
in my way
or in me...
There's no highway
to the head of Gwen Cee,
There's bricks and concrete......
slabs
and memories
from the mags....

Magnolia homes that is...
Same color as the bricks
which once stood between Jefferson and Ali
I didn't ask for this ish

It was given to me

This skin…
A barrier,
a burden
apparently
a question
everybody wants to ask me or assume

Everybody wants to judge me
"Oh, she think she hood cause she got that baby"
My response, with a laugh…
'Sweetie I am who I am and who I was from 79 not 2003'
"Hood" is relatable
It is consistency
A known piece…
of someone…
Ingrained interpretation…

August 2, 2015

The Eyes

Cee

What the Heart

Feels

"Fine-As-Hell"

I wear it
because it's
enduring like a seashell,

Golden color
comforts me;
Makes me feel
Fine-As-Hell.

Three years in the making;
Convincing is the tale
you tell,
Longing, desire...
wanting but not saying;

I love that your story
intrigued me
and established
Fine-As-Hell.

Drink the drink, taste it,
Not wasted;
But definitely no way to bail,
This is the moment to become certain! Yes or No! On that
which I refer to as Fine-As-Hell.

Thank you for your action: grab, pull close, hold tight;
ensuring my plan would not fail,
Thirty minutes of fun, make the most, because in life,
sometimes it's just that once
But applying light memories of heavy moments makes it all
Fine-As-Hell.

Your lips speak, no words to hear; it's the emotion on
which I dwell,
Words--unheard but statements made; Lips felt, not
overrated,

It's…
that…
Fine-As-Hell.

On and on, certain number of days, 1,698 of these and
hours and hours, longing to see, engaging feelings as the
heart's ideas leaked
Out into the world,

Our world, black and white faded to gray…

As we forget to protect members of our society
Continue to engage in this combat, why would we ever do
that?
Getting into the mind; seeing the enemy and the lover but
not quite ready to hit that nail into the coffin
of a potential life succumbing
to lustful death,

The foundation around the coffin is empty, transparency is
ours,
There is no memory which to cling; though it is guaranteed,
soon to be…
Fine-As-Hell.

May, 2013

"La Familia"

Yes, we are busy but that does not mean you should not ask,
We don't live in the same house,
So does that mean we are not part of the equation or have the same tasks?
Such as celebrating or honoring a loved one or experiencing "quality" time hanging out?
Of course, we should be part of the task, the goal shouldn't be the event or the food but the gathering of family.
La Familia, last time I checked, the importance was "the family."
Facebook posts and all these damn quotes stating that loyalty is what makes you family,
That may be the case because blood seems questionable…
I don't understand why including "everyone" is not acceptable.
How can we claim to be a family? When constantly left out? Sure when the stress is up family is there but what about a regular Tuesday or a coffee on the deck, what about when it's my own Daddy's birthday or a "get your hair did par-tay?"

No invite; ignited instead.
Chest hurting, throbbing head…
Adrenaline from emotion of being hurt
What is so bad about us? Is it "us" or our kids?
Please someone answer this…

It makes no sense…
That we are not relative to our relatives…
Forces me to just stop by and drop off a gift bag or a gift card,
That does not offer the same form of quality, time is tight –

Yes, it is……………hard…
But no one knows if we can take part…

Without asking, instead the burden continues to lie with the heart.

I hate to think of all the things they miss, someday the loneliness--- that will exist; missed... opportunities to build bonds like seen on commercials selling oatmeal pies.

Fam time is not just "party on the hill" and Christmas.

Tired of being outed, constantly by these lack of inclusions, delusions that say "family is not all inclusive."
When in fact, it is.

There's no picking and choosing.
There's no competition; no winning...

Just a lost world...

Mankind losing.

February 27, 2014

"Addicted"

I understand now.....what it is to feel that way,
I understand the treacherous feelings of an addict;
unstoppable in night and day.
I never felt anything like that before...
Now the need pelts like pouring rain...
it won't leave me making me feel insane...
I never knew that high; that crave; that fiend...
Although I claimed too...
Judging the person's addiction...
claiming to...but not really understanding the pain....
being inflicted...onto them...
Not just the pain but that CRAVE!!!! That need!!!!
To have it.... to breathe....
The life it gives; like oxygen,
the thrilling high......inside the mind, resulting from between
the thighs...
the sensation to the body making the world seem perfect....
The lit spirit...
Feeling no further need for soul searching...
That "everything is right; I'm not sick..."
Those longings to embrace.....
what was once the moment...
To chase......... It because you know nothing else but to
want it....
Twenty four years of written poems, jail letters that
expressed sentiment....
Writings which I thought said it all....
But I realize now, until a true understanding of addiction is
developed nothing matters
because the experience.....
was never as intense....
as staled.......now hated......
because the high is lost,
it can't be found...
So lips rough,
hands shaking,
looking like hell...

because heart beats rapidly and then slow...
eyes wide open and then closed....
Rest. Can't rest! Who needs sleep? Emotions or lack
thereof..... Penetrating maliciously the blood......
That to the heart pumps.....
That deep sickness and urgency through....
Heart! Beat!
That high!!!!
Where is it! I need it?
I have this expectation...and YOU,
You must feed it!
You owe this to the one who loves you.....
You chose to serve me severely and in its severity....is this
"ish" you have inflicted...
like wicked....sex driven by the devil....
Severely!!!
So now you can't stop...
Tantalizing; ends don't exist....
Cycles recycle themselves...
There is no end in sight....
because in hindsight, I see and these insides tell
me...more of your senses are needed....
Hear. Feel. Touch. Fulfill me!
Be trill as you taste me....
Thrill me because our "we..."
must be......a lifelong pursuit.
I know nothing else beyond that high,
I see this high you deliver,
my heart melts,
My mind relaxes to a state of coma..
Legs feel weightless....
and I shift...
To see you first...
causing my stomach to drop; gulping a swallow...
then allowing you to rain in my veins.
Sadly you've never been a straight shooter...
Nor have I ever been able to say no...
"Let me go! Oh, wait please don't!"
Make me fiend for you...Lean on you...

Suck it up and go to that land where I dream of you...
Make me take you,
make me shake,
Raise the stakes....adamantly.
No contemplating!!!
Because I now understand that fiend,
that life!
Never thought I'd be chasing that first high.
That I'd live for "it"
Not using the mind behind these eyes....
because that mind chooses to sit aside....
Seated in a race to the top....
Highest victory....
Needing that high...
Not glorifying any drug....
but understanding the addiction of such...
because you fu@$!ng love too good...
Today that ish is love...
Your loving is drugging.....
Love in me...to me...through me...
Love do me.... As I chase the first high I ever felt.....That is
you...

Summer, 2014

"Gorgeous"

Trying
Spying
Denying
Crying
Now cut eyes eyeing
Not buying
Into it anymore, not sighing
But breath released
Broken heart's last beat, not dying
Now healed, strength intensifying
Rain water drenches
Fist clenches
Body found in trenches
With traces of you
MIA, DNA, DOA
Prisoner of your grip
Tears flow, no drip
Flowing, drenched.
In an instant
You vanish
The disadvantaged
Your truth while lying
All that's been done, sky seen
Two greater than one?
Not in quality
Gorgeous split personality
Did I kill or die......Me?

April 2, 2015

"Puppet Master"

Depressed.
She wants to stalk him because his talk is thin,
Nearly shredded, because he lays it on thick but spreads
it...so thin......... many women............claiming to have
him
And so the chores start to show
And even more, his indecisiveness begins to faintly glow;
Red flag, whispers to her then speaks aloud
Yelling, "I am unavailable; what you see is not what you
get"
"I have strings attached to many...........
I am the puppet master"
"However, I love what you spit
but not enough to reach levels..............
of dedication....you better be patient........
Walk on them shells
As I continue to play with you -- toy"
"Cause my body which appears and my hands that feel
like that of a grown man hide my ambiguity
like the dark'
"Nothing about me is transparent as you believe
The only transparency is the holes you see in my
fragments, loose encounters
and words that lift you up and serve you like downers."

May 7, 2015

"Pot of Chili"

Standing over
Stirring chili that I just added spice and water to
Wondering why I allowed myself to return to you
Yet again

Because I am empty on the inside, lacking nourishment
But you're the spoon.... that stirs my emotions

No encouragement
To leave
because when I do
You make promises you do not intend
to keep..................
and
though, my disappointment fades and my anger cools

My crisis lingers
I continue to starve
And starve
And starve

I crave things that you can't give
Because that one hundred time written about
unwillingness...

Inside of you
Makes it impossible for you to cherish
The wife
In me

As this pot of chili becomes warmed again
My cheek does too

As this single tear
Grazes my face
Salt taste
Given you 18 – 38

125

That's twenty years

I gave up my home girls; salt water; island
Myself...

For a relationship who's consistency
Cannot even compete
With that of my damn pot of chili....

May 16, 2015

"Her Purse"

No designer name necessary for her purse...
Her purse is often far more than what it appears...

It could be her medicine cabinet,
the diaper bag for her children,
It may house temporary snacks, serving as her only
kitchen
it could be the temporary place which holds her soul and
spirit....
when they so badly need lifting....

So her purse is so much more,

Some large, some small, some bright, some neutral in
tone,
Sometimes a replication of her character as it represents a
choice she was able to make on her own.

Often, the only thing she can grab beyond her children
when escaping home.
And, sometimes not, as it's left behind...

And, when she's burdened by heavy disturbance on her
shoulders, mind unable to grasp, physically and
emotionally hurting,
Seemingly alone in this entire world...
her purse is so much more,

it can be a sense of "I will survive"
And "I will be.......all right"
and a place for her to put all of the things that she needs
to hold so tight...to protect her being, and that of her
children...
her purse.........is "hers."
For all its internal findings, broken or mended, outspoken
or hidden,
In times of weakness or strength, It is often all she has

beyond the clothes which flank her skin,
In times when only a stranger is there to serve as family or
friend,
It is her familiar, it is her control
It is a sign of "survive" for a better tomorrow...

As the contents change over time;
Transitional housing, transit tickets,
badge for a new job, apartment key, utility...
bill in...her name,
new car key fob....

She does too,

Ever-changing.

August 2, 2015

From the Life of

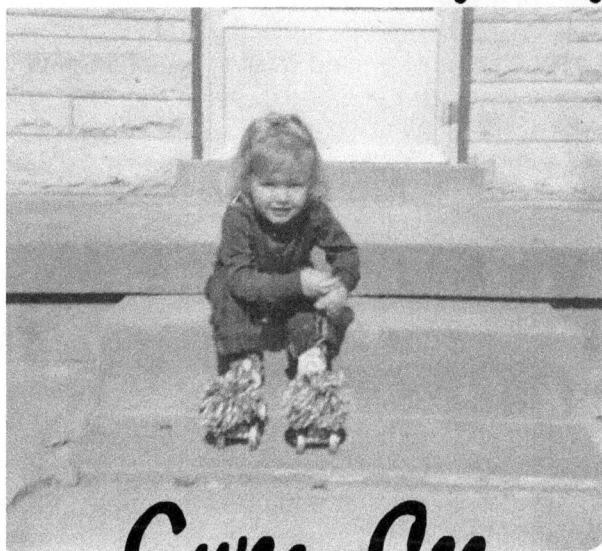

Gwen Cee

"Madness of Cee"

In the midst of what she seen, two toothpicks stabbed into foreheads,
Her hands free phone hidden in her closet because when things got loud, she knew she had to call for help.

Every time the Galveston Island PD and occasionally the SWAT team would arrive, you would cry.
Your heart hurt, I know it did; you were devastated by how you were living your one life.

And, that one time, when you went to grab her, your little girl because you knew she had to be calling 911... I know still to this day, I know still that you've never forgiven yourself for the pee that ran down her leg...

The fear that you bestowed upon her when you came to take her into that room where the angel you'd been beating sat
She is no longer mad that she attended four schools in one year: Rosenberg, Alamo, San Jacinto and Burnett...

She was a hostage of her own mind as well as held hostage; sometimes kept away from school, missing the TX Assessment Test at the end of the semester, but with no negotiation she was still one of the best... She was still placed in all honors classes as a Ball High School Tornado...
All while within her, was a tornado; turmoil, she wished a hurricane would hit her island and "take him" or "her" out.

Galveston Island Police Department on the scene, but those same officers did nothing... They didn't do anything to remove her from those terribles, unbearables, unthinkables...
Yes, those same ones I spoke of in the past, when you encouraged me to turn the page.

Let me tell you, I'm not here just to speak words, I'm not here to just words from this page...
I'm here to tweak words, to rewrite a broken past, no reluctance, as I recast a memory from then to a new... image

So that I can see myself in a new light, I'm here to finally be freed from what has been haunting me my whole life... 25 to life, is what it seems, Post-Traumatic Stress, to hell with that-- I want to win.

I'm the daughter but I have forgiven my father...
So, why do I still live it daily?
I fear! That I am not good enough; that no one will accept me because...My life wasn't perfect...
Without that jerk in it... Does not mean I would have had a perfect life...but just because I didn't come from a certain neighborhood, a perfect home full of love, a Pleasantville place, full of quiet and nonviolent space...

Just because I lived at 2813 Sunny Lane......doesn't mean I can't overcome those 1,095 gloomy days.

Those are memories, I have forgiven my father, Forgiven him for all of the women he chose to beat.
Because he didn't mean...
to do this with the watching of my eyes, Oh I know he did not realize...the impact it would have upon me...the little girl and the adult me...

I know he never thought as woman, I'd live unhappily, carry the burden of my childhood, and argue with my husband on a daily basis, when things should be "all good"
...
As I look back, I wished for Face-off like Nick Cage.... I see my different faces at age 8, age 10 age 13.... Even if he wanted a boy; he didn't mean to do these things to me...

But you know those beatings and sharp edges, burdens and angles were sent to me...
Those women were my angels, not my angles...
See, I used to see them as burdens and angles and hard points to get around...
But now I see those women...they were "angels,"
He beat them; they showed me who I could never allow myself to be!
Bodies like graffiti; bruises; Purple, Blue, Green, the size of grapefruit...

Once my bedroom wall tumbled down, completely, as an angel flew through...

I'm not saying my father is a bad man, because no one is perfect, we don't choose to be jerks...It's... just the drugs, overcame him, twisted his mind and somehow he was deeply intrigued by the use of his own supply.

Hurricane Alicia in 1984 had nothing on him; the first time, I think I was two, it was November, I remember...a bloody nose...
But I have forgiven you my father!
And, I see now that it's time to forgive myself; stop holding grudges and discriminating against my background...

We all come from different experiences and events, some inspiring, some minimal,
I'm not waiting for karma or payback, I recommend everyone to forgive someone who toward them has been criminal...

See, I know I am not the one to judge you father, I'm not a prize but I was your child,
I'm far from perfect; I can't claim to understand...
I can only imagine the misery which engulfed your heart and mind for so many years...

A bright darkness with opposition, torturous

When the time came I did not sit on the jury...
The regret from which you suffered and each time you
heard from them...
That you caused serious bodily harm; With Angel Lori...
It was "four hours of photos and eight rolls of film."
I know you didn't want to be that man; the drugs had
control of you, your mind, your body and your hands.

You merely lived the madness of that man.

Summer, 2013

"Diamonds & Rocks"

She's been through diamonds and rocks
But her pigment is her flaw
She does not fit in.
Went through bus stops, beating graffiti blocks but she
does not fit in.
"Raised" (term questionable) by dope dealing father... door
kicked in; Galveston Swat Team's best...

Taking photos and filters for the disc
Saying these should be in grayscale so she don't get
dissed

Because she does not fit in

Even though it's who she is
It's who she's always been, it's part of her past, and to this
game she is not new...
No fu@k!#$ blast, no onstage trying to be "down" with the
crew type shit this is

And, when you don't let her in
It's the unbelievable denier denying of something so
important, pushing her down, weighing on her making her
feel like she has no worth
Because she doesn't have anywhere else to turn,

This is her life, who she is, who she's always freaking been

In the silence
In the moment
of truth, she remembers the violence

Struggles from Clarksdale
Living through
Damitrius Strong
Even with "strong" tatted on her chest
She has found weakness

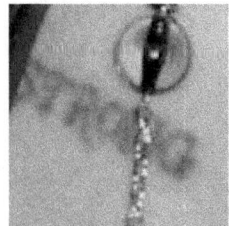

134

She knows that this is who she is,

She's reached her ultimate…

She will survive any malicious prosecution against her
She will survive the invasion and the cleaning of the
community that she associates herself with

She will do as she preaches on to herself, which she will
finally uplift…

Based on the description of where she comes from, she
does fit in…

Let's see:
Is she doing the same thing that you want to do on a daily
basis?
Ambitious all hours not just 8 – 5,
Faced with raising respectful children
And worry about what will happen to 1 out of every three,
And every day after worry about her children getting shot
by the officers,
Those "sworn to protect folks"

And, she has her own drive; pedaling to impact community
Because what is now just whack only appears to be getting
worse, more death, more fear, more hurt
She too is a mother with the ability to guide and lead;
shape and lean
Hard on them to keep them straight…

So, just because she doesn't read or spit her poetry as
comfortably as some

Doesn't mean that she doesn't have something to give
To change the life of just one,
Single individual, any
Or impact so many

Because of the life she has lived

She has been unbreakable,
when she should have been broken,

She has knowledge that should have been taken,

But see God chose to grant it to her
To use for other things and so her knowledge should be let
in…Words Accepted!

February 26, 2015

"Acceptance"

So............It should have been expected,

That I'd never be accepted,
But when you neglected...

Me and my words of poetry

Or when you refuse me because I'm married to him,
Well, when you do that you are no different from them,

"Them," those folks who "look" more similar to me

But refuse to let me in,
Number of friends limited,
Acquaintances by the many...

When they want something from me, a resume or job
coaching they ask
But in all actuality they don't understand how I write, not
one piece of poetry, not a goal, not one single task.

They have nothing in common with me; they don't
understand me
Therefore, they use me when my skills are handy.

Poetry? You get it.

Ambition? You got it

Words written to lift, out of love, out of struggle
But your acceptance of me? You've fought it.

Seems as though, I'm expected to keep to my "kind,"
But my "kind" never accepted the person who sees with
these brown eyes,

They don't understand my poetry, thoughts, challenges or rhymes,
You don't and really won't know me, because my...

Face or appearance doesn't align
with what you believe I should look like
for what I speak

It's not your problem though, for it is...
MY
burden...

February 28, 2015

Short Poem in Life of Gwen Cee

Refusal to support me
Failure of your heart
Embrace my tone and voice, ART.

April 21, 2015

"Girl Undone"

It's the effect of my...
personality,
That after 22 years he
remembers the first time...
he.......laid his eyes
upon me...
It's the tone of my voice, innocently,
A young lady.
That makes him recall exactly when he asked for my
number...
White shirt, touch of red, and tennis shoes,
size nine waist, jeans, fitted on my teen curves,
Long brown hair permed; "Make-up less" same as
current...
Down for whatever, protected by the home girls,
Who always rode with...
This laid back, "never discuss a feeling" chic...
But always "feeling" something intense,
Hearing the words of Prince, rewriting the songs to better
fit....And give...An accurate description...
Ocean waves, salt water, girl undone.
Little white tercel, the corvette,
Riding to T. Naps,
The entire island...Was ours...
Cherry Hill, Boone's Farm,
Embellished moments...No limits.
Endless. Erotic. Summer.

June 8, 2015

Think Like a Man;
Cee His Perspective

"Gemini" aka "Thuggish Ruggish Bone"

When you say you are stressed because of your work, hurt
and dirt.
You are referring to me.
I am your work,
I am your hurt,
and fa' damn sho' ya dirt!

It's my witty intelligence, eloquence, the smile on my
face...
When I enter the room you think of great love and when I
touch you –
You feel great lust!
All things become hazed...

What you didn't know and I didn't allow you to see is this
intellect,

This intellect that makes it nearly impossible for you to
keep me.
My attention moves so quick, I need new stimuli,
While you are falling in love with me and my d!@%...
I'm often off, ready for something new, which I must try.

I am so damn charming that you will write, characterizing
me in your poetry and
saying the same thing in many different ways.
I'll be your notebook, game changer, tangle you in a web
where there is no escape...

You will fight but because I can be whatever you want me
to be in the moment,

You won't be able to get away... so you will make a
resolution, say you are too smart
and not understand why you are chasing this dumb ish...
But all along I will say just the right phrase,

Spark just the right nerve, make you
lust....................when you need it the most
because......

I am that guy...
That thuggish ruggish bone!!!!
That Gemini! That after you first googled – you should
have left alone...

I'm going to help you grow, I bring harmony...
I bring inspiration, you will write and perform because I
give you so much to say...

But my curious mind that had you open up, when you start
to love me it will shut
Then I'm going to expose you and see how you tick,
And once I have you all figured out...

My need to shift will kick, my love of new things will take
over...

It's my weakness...
And you being the Libra that you are – yeah, you are going
to fight so hard......

To try to tweak my interest,

You are going to run yourself into the ground as you try to
"create" more...... us...
Not less.

Then I'm going to feel forced
And then I will shut down, keeping you lined up, saying you
was my ace but you
needed to slow down cause I can't move at your pace.

See, I'm a Gemini and therefore,
I can be heartbreaking.

The sensual touches from me, the bitten lip, the tender kiss and the gentle tug of
your hair - yeah that one right there was really a tug at your heart – at that very
moment you became mine – for the time.

But this Gemini tossed you to the left – to the side
But YOU, Little Miss Libra believes what you write becomes life.

Thought you could show love and make me alright,
Thought you could be a visionary for me, providing sight
Thought you could break these invisible walls, with all your might

Little Miss Libra wouldn't walk away, got on my damn nerves,

I was done.

But kept you on board with few words…
Because you are a Libra and a poet, a combination that endangers…

You seek balance in all things, overanalyzing all words,
How easy it was to keep your mind a blur,

A little riddle here, a one liner every now and then that insinuated I see you in

my future; that we would ever go further than we once were…

See when I wanted to meet you, tried for a month, you were exciting and new,

I had no plan for us…so after I met you by a second chance…

And after we advanced...

And you succumbed to the touch of these hands
Baby girl, I could go on for days – about the many ways of
how a Gemini loves to play.

Libras are our best match!

And as Gemini, I'm going to always keep you on your
toes until you put your feet flat, turn your back and walk
away.

Good luck with that and...

Since we know that won't happen...
Get more notebooks, and you are going to need some
ink...

Lil Miss Libra Poet – that resolution you made – you might
want to rethink!

Like you said, I am your eyelids when you go to sleep at
night,

The secretion I spit is what puts you on that mic,
You've been real competitive, trying to win me but
remember as a Gemini, I'm a risk,

I say anything I need to get what I want, you are my
sidekick...
who fell in love – like Juvy said "makes them smart chics
sick...'

I appreciate that you are a ride or die.........
Who wants to be on my team...

But as a Gemini......
One of my greatest fears is boredom and routine.
Little Miss Libra you now know you can't fix me.

You cannot suck me in with your words,
Your ink pen does not put venom in me as my gentle bite
to your lip does you…
You cannot "make me fall in love"

Because I am a Gemini,
your thuggish ruggish bone…

As much as you want us to be inseparable,

I can't be your man, your dude or ya patnah!
Because I must experience my world…
on my own.

July 3, 2014

"The End"

She knows it's her sin
And she will continue to read the ten
Commandments and pray for a way to decline him

But her addiction and the need to have him is all she thinks
about
She knows nothing else
Because two years ago, what she knew – he blocked
What she knew would be – was stopped
What she predicted would come – came
And what she predicted would speak – spoke
And what she predicted would rise – rose

And then there was this...
Gut wrenching knot
This low down dirty blow
Because it came to be and it became known
And it became known.........that he was not
The rise that she thought
The inspiration she sought
The man she craved...
And so she became
restless ......
and she started wandering
Physically around
Searching for something or someone else,
to take that place
To fill that void
To replay what she done with him
Time and time and time again

She finds herself replaying ----
And it works so great......the first kiss...
Senseless but so soft
Just makes...
her want to melt away
The first caress of the face
The first time she feels beautiful in his arms

It all works because what she's looking for is the adventure
that he first brought to her
When he first lurked…
Watching her from afar
Speaking to her
Brushing up against her gently
Incredibly
She's become someone she would normally despise

Because she's going here and there and even there and
maybe even there
To chase the look that was in his eyes
The first time he made her write…

He basically put the pen in her hand and said "you are
going to write about me"

"I'm going to allow you to know enough of me and to feel
me and to understand me and to love me and to need me
and to thrive for me,

So that you will write about me, "I need a book" that will
describe my life, my past, my sorrows, my pains, my
neglect, the way that I've treated you and all others…"
"What I want you to do also, is write about my mother, it
will all be included - you're going to write about me…"

And he,

Touched her, opened her palm as she melted in his palm
He placed the pen in her hand and she began to write
And when that piece was done she wrote again
And when that piece was done, he would give her more,
just enough, one thrust

Here, there, more lust,

Until…

She completed the book…

He was done at that point

Because what he needed
She had completed

Therefore, the pages
of what she thought was forever, new stages
to come
with
so many opportunities to play
the role she longed for
and prepared for,

Like a play with numerous ending, gets multiple re-invents…

those pages had no permanence,

Instead the curtains closed permanently signaling the complete emptiness of 'the end.'

May 28, 2015

Faith that He Cees Me

"Conquer"

I've given up the fight,
Because I know that {place} too has oxygen.
I've given up the fight,
The fear; what if {might}
Because I know that in
the end
truth shall triumph.
And that truth,
Is that I need not fear,
I am protected.
In each breath, each blink,
each concern,
each tear...drop...
Protected through it all;
no more worry or sorrow;
458 missed tomorrows...
Because I have lost
the fight in me...
after more than two years.
I've given up the fight...
Opted for his might.
Like she {Gwen Cee} once wrote, "leave, live worry free,
live simple days..."
I've given up the fight; the burden that it has been, the
anxiety-driven, aging mess, sickness, worthless worry,
NO more fret...I've let it go,
I've given up the fight...realizing it is not within my power
or up to me to
"conquer" on my own...

January 27, 2015

"Carry Me Away"

I found this post; Thought it was disturbing
See when you're friends, you never conjure the idea that it may end,
Then years later you see her shout to an angel through poetry…
Her memory, a beautiful thing…
One of which you never even knew,
Because the drama of life intervened…
And that best friendship "forever," the one that seemed…
Bonded by your Libra characteristics and a love of FDDP…
The one of similar styles and wonderfully shared traits…
Yes, that friendship lost its way, came apart…
But the core of it, the heart, still exists…
And so my friend,
I saw your post today…
Your words written in a way, beautiful.
And now I know of your pain,
With tears and out of love I write for you…
Because a friendship never dies when it is true.
I cannot imagine your loss,
And, while I know you have a circle of folks who's care for you is deep,
Your K and your M, I still care and your reflection brought me to weep.
You are blessed with an Angel,
Just like I was once blessed…
To be your best…Friend,
My friend.

March 31, 2015

"Faith"

Alone…Isolated
happilyHATED
Broken…Binged
lightlyWEIGHTED
He carries me
Worry….decrease
Then cease.
Faith.

APRIL 30, 2015

"Self-Reflect"

I self reflect so
hard...
I mirror me.

My past nags...
like a two way
mirror

Watching me bare...
My soul.

Baggage gone, I let it go.

Accelerated, dust in the rear view,

I despise the mirror's sheer truth.

June 10, 2015

"Amidst a Kiss"

She seeks attention,

Not to fill a void,
Not to replace something that once was but is now missin,
But to replace something that is broken.

She searches for repair,
Finds it in a glimpse of her stare,
Reading His word, heart touching, as soft as…
a shoulder caress;
Similar to joy when surprised with a kiss…

Burdens lift…
Themselves…
When these moments are found.

She seeks attention,
To remedy a loneliness,
One that she allowed,
By fearing loss of what she thought would mount…
To a kind of sacred love.
She seeks attention,
In places she originally would dare not be,
In reality,
In syllables heard,
Through defining words,
Which vary in meaning,

In places, where space is…
Already cramped,
Inside a heart that has no true room,
One that is now ready to be amped

Through love never known, to be shown…
the way

She seeks attention,

As she learns her way to her eternal home

In the integrity of what is delivered by words written based on His lips,

Landing in His...
Palm,

His hand guides her,

His feet lead,

She follows...

She finds attention today,

Through faith in tomorrow.

June 9, 2015

La Isla Bonita

Life Near the Cee

"Island of G."

That place with its
nighttime stars dripping
over the sand
and
they fall like part of the ocean
and I can't seem to escape the chains that I felt
that made me drop at my knees
the ocean waves, the cool breeze
79 degrees

Dropping

slightly at nights to about seventy.

It's that island
that place that made you feel like you were stuck with
chains
that made you feel like you shall drop to your knees
because of that heart wrench memory
it was a part of you…

For it, you would sink into the sand
Be stung
by fire ants
Be burned by sun
Reflecting off the ocean: highlighting the backdrop of the
seawall

The Gulf flowing freely
Your emotions deeply
Intertwined like seaweed
Engulfed you easily can be

Lost at sea…
in a mirage made of shells, treasure of the ocean
and your broken segments
Faded by the island tide

Washed away
Stolen

The island

greater than all gold, cash and immaculate tokens
In its "greatest" it's a dreaded...desired world treasure

Its air; the madness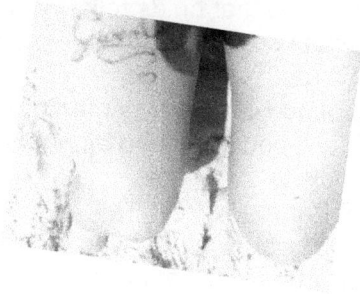

Just the island of G

    Chain you down

        Salt water life

           Island bound

               April 4, 2015

"A Place"

A place that I must bear witness to,
A place that I most fear,
A place offering peaceful sounds which ring what's
become KY
Acquainted ears,
A place that holds folks who aren't bound,
Who were once and still are so dear.....
To me...
A place of long ago memories
More powerful than all human sensory
A place
of trauma
That would school you at Ball,
Granted you got out of Central...
A place that didn't mislead us
In our mischievous
A place that protected us in our doings,

Giving us safety.
Rebuttals
to the negatives we were pursuing
Enhancing our hasty....
Terrible decisions,
perfectly envisioned...
by us know it all Golden Eagles.
A place of growth, redesign, devastation,
and culmination...
Of beauty after Ike,
of challenge, of strength...
overcoming teen pregnancy and street fights.
A place that is a small knot; heavy like an anchor; well
known by

those endearing
All of it's wide open views,
Highs and lows,
Tropical blows,
Neighboring nose,
The "who did this" and "guess who knows"
The salt sometimes thrown...
A place of survival,
Sunrise unconditional,
A place of granular friendships,
No regrets,
except when
your exit...
Has...been...too...long.

April 5, 2015

www.ingramcontent.com/pod-product-compliance
Lightning Source LLC
Chambersburg PA
CBHW060443040426
42331CB00044B/2537